TIPPY, TIPPY, TAP, WHICH TIP DO YOU WANT?

SELF CARE TIPS

ANJU ANAND

Made with ♥ on the Notion Press Platform
www.notionpress.com

DEDICATED TO

MY LOVING FAMILY

BOTH IN INDIA AND CANADA

*WITHOUT WHOSE SUPPORT MY BOOK
AND I WOULD NOT BE COMPLETE.*

Contents

Contents

Contents

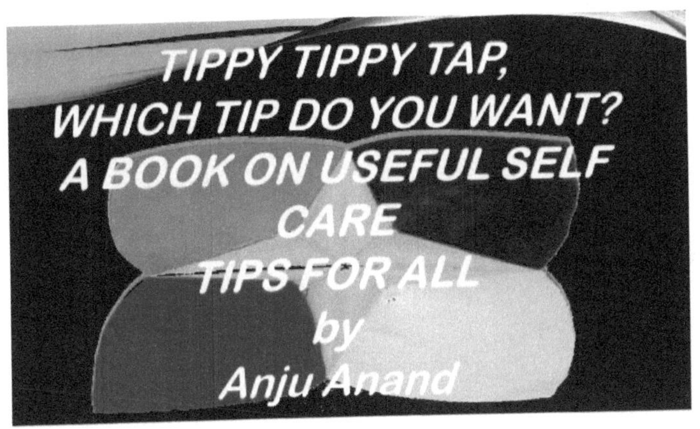

TIPS ARE MANY, CHOICE IS YOURS.

Preface

WE ARE SCALING OUR PEAKS

There are Mt Everest, Kanchenjunga, and Mt Blanc within all of us,

We have to scale our peaks without any fuss.

When the conditions are good we cover a good distance,

Sometimes all on our own without any assistance.

But there are times when the conditions are adverse,

And we climb with moods perverse.

We climb, we skid, we fall, we drift,

At times not even allow ourselves pitilessness or short shrift.

Some mountaineers are ahead of me, some behind me,

Some toiling and others making climbing a perpetual spree.

At the juncture I stand, I am looking up towards some and looking down upon others,

The rays of the mountain sun radiate many colors.

Storms, avalanches, and blizzards will all be there,

But not reaching the top will be so unfair.

There is no going back before scaling my summit,

Now that I am inching my way to the top, there is no way that I can plummet.

There is no way that I can plummet, the climb must go on,

On reaching the top of my peak will I be able to rest thereupon?

Here we are all fighting our own battles, scaling our mountain peaks.

All our struggles are not the same but the **LAW OF SURVIVAL OF THE FITTEST** applies to all.

I once read somewhere—FOR HOW LONG ONE CAN BE ON AUTO MODE, ONE HAS TO TAKE CONTROL.

So I have penned down some thoughts, some suggestions, some tips, some ideas that I gathered on my journey as a daughter, a wife, a mother, a daughter–in–law, a teacher and, a human being as to how to care for oneself.

I have tried to include some very real-life instances also—trying to be all-inclusive.

Most of what you will find may be relatable, you may have read it somewhere, heard it, or, experienced it, which means that though we may not be in the same boat, we are in the same storm. We have to brace this storm together, so while we are there, why don't we learn from our experiences?

Acknowledgements

- I am thankful to my son Kushagr Anand who worked day in and day out with me, helping me with formatting, proof reading, editing, inserting pictures, etc.

- If you are reading this, then it means that you have taken out some time from your busy schedule to have a look at my book. I appreciate your effort and am grateful to you that you are ready to explore what the book contains. My sincere thanks to my readers and well-wishers.

- My sincere thanks to Dr. Omatee Ann Marie Hansraj of Wordsmith International Editorial, who helped me to take my first step in the literary world.

OUR MIND IS LIKE A PARACHUTE

Hello humble souls reading/viewing this--
PONDER OVER THIS
OUR MIND IS LIKE A PARACHUTE
IT WILL WORK ONLY WHEN WE OPEN IT

PARACHUTE IF OPENED IS A LIFE SAVIOR, BUT WHAT IF IT DOESN'T OPEN?

Yes, it is true.

If we take decisions with an open mind, when we work with an open mind, only then will we be able to survive the everyday tensions, strife, and agonies, which happen to be a part of everyone's life--yours as well as mine.

WE CAN'T REMAIN AUTO-MODE CHARACTERS FOREVER--SOONER OR LATER, WE HAVE TO TAKE CHARGE OF OUR LIVES.

WE ARE OUR OWN ALLADIN'S GENIE.

IF THERE IS ANYONE WHO IS AIMING TO MAGICALLY APPEAR AND SUDDENLY MAKE OUR LIFE BETTER, IT IS NONE OTHER THAN US.

WE ARE YOUR OWN ALLADIN'S GENIE.

WE ARE IN THE SAME STORM

WE ARE IN THE SAME STORM

Someone has rightly said that we are not in the same boat but in the same storm.

Together, we sail in grace into the world we transform.

Some of us are in schooners, some are in brigs.

Barks, yet others in galleons,

All at sea surrounded by halcyons.
Some of us have entered the sea recently.
While others have been floating there ceaselessly.
But now all of us have been hit by the storm.
The challenge of challenging the norm entices us to change our destiny.
Small boats may sail through while large ships may sink.
It all depends on our ability to ponder, plan and think.
Storms will come and storms will pass.
But we must remember that at the end of every storm, there is a rainbow.
Life's storms too can be endured with grit, patience, and determination.
And only then will we be able to earn everyone's admiration.

ONLY THE BRAVE WILL SAIL THROUGH

All of us as human beings have to face a lot of struggles in our lives. The intensity and proportions may vary, but struggles are always present.

We are all like ships in a storm, all in the middle of the sea, waiting for the storm to abate so that we can anchor safely.

For some of us, the struggle has just begun, while others have been struggling for a long time. At the end of the day what matters is our patience, our forbearance, and our positivity. We should not think in terms of giving up or quitting. Every struggle of ours should be considered a stepping stone to success.

Advocating for or sticking up for oneself should never be considered 'being tough'.

One is entitled to have difficult emotions, to alter one's opinion, to disagree, to express discomfort, and to not always be comfortable with what is going on around us.

As long as our ships/boats/vessels are strong enough, we'll be able to sail through. In other words, we can only look after others if we first look after ourselves.

One should accept oneself as one is. This is the most difficult thing because it stands against one's training, education, and even culture.

From the very beginning, one is always told how one should be. Nobody has ever been told that one is worthy of what one is.

Self-care must precede the care of others.

CELEBRATE YOURSELF. NO ONE EXCEPT YOU IS AWARE OF WHAT IT TAKES TO BE YOU.

CHAPTER THREE

THE MISSING TILE SYNDROME

THE MISSING TILE SYNDROME

Hi Dear readers,
Look carefully at the mosaic of tiles above.

What do you notice?

A very unique design for some?

For others, a combination of white, grey, or black?

A ribboned design for yet some others?

But one thing that all of you must have noticed is the tile that is not there.

YES, THE MISSING TILE MUST HAVE CAUGHT YOUR ATTENTION.

RIGHT?

Some of you must have noticed it immediately.

Some others might have noticed it after a while or as a matter of fact/casually.

Exactly. Our eyes and our minds are very quick to see/ point out missing things.

We waste our energy and time wondering why the tile is missing. Is it by chance?

Is it broken?

Will it be repaired?

As a result, we don't remember taking time out to appreciate the design, the color combination, and the intricate way in which the tiles have been arranged. We also don't remember appreciating the arduous work put in by the Masons, the laborers, etc.

Since the rest of the flooring is flawless, one's gaze is drawn to that single missing tile!

The "missing tile syndrome" has been coined for this situation.

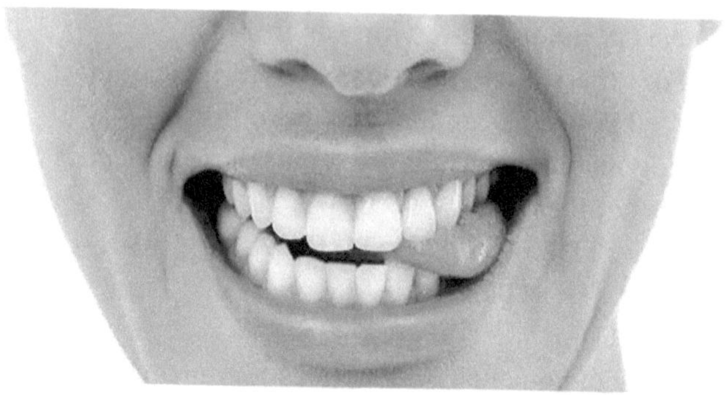

THE TONGUE ALWAYS REACHES OUT FOR THE SPACE WHERE THE TOOTH ONCE STOOD

Why is it that it is so natural that after a tooth extraction, our tongue always reaches out for the space where the tooth once stood? (The missing tooth)

Similarly, as parents and instructors, we only notice the problematic features of a child—yelling, tantrums, bullying, lying, whining, and so on.

Our attention is quickly drawn to the absence of appropriate behavior. We waste time and energy focusing on his negative triggers rather than appreciating his positive qualities or traits.

We need to look below the surface, to find out the reasons for his behavior, and use positive reinforcement to correct his negative behaviors.

TRY TO IGNORE THE NEGATIVE TRAITS OF YOUR CHILD

The phrase "Missing Tile Syndrome" was invented by Dennis Prager. By focusing solely on what we are missing, we deny ourselves the happiness and enjoyment of what we have.

The MISSING SYNDROME diverts our attention and inhibits us from remaining peaceful and content. We spend a lot of time regretting what we don't have rather than appreciating and expressing gratitude for what we do have.

TRY TO IGNORE THE NEGATIVE TRAITS OF YOUR CHILD

WE ARE FOREVER HAUNTED BY WHAT IS MISSING FROM OUR LIFE, RATHER THAN BEING CONTENT WITH WHAT WE HAVE.

CHAPTER FOUR

WE CANNOT ALWAYS STEER CLEAR OF TOXIC PEOPLE, BUT WE CAN AVOID THEIR PERNICIOUS INFLUENCE.

I THINK NO ONE CAN MAKE US FEEL INFERIOR, LOW, OR USELESS, WITHOUT OUR CONSENT.

If we allow people to treat us like doormats, they will treat us exactly that way.
But if we stand up for ourselves, then there is no mat for them to step on.

ALWAYS REMEMBER—A SHIP NEVER SINKS IN WATER BUT SINKS ONLY WHEN WATER ENTERS IT.

So what I am trying to say is - We all are social animals and need to interact with several people during the day and throughout our lives. We cannot avoid people. Many people that we come into contact with are not conducive to our mental peace—they are TOXIC.

It could be anyone—for some—a bossy parent, a rude/ moody offspring, an overcritical boss, or a boastful neighbor.

They will always be there—pulling you down, demeaning you, hurting you. However, you are safe - you will sail—AS LONG AS YOU DO NOT ALLOW THEIR NEGATIVITY TO GNAW AT YOU.

But the minute you take the bait, you are finished. If you let negativity act on you like a termite, you will be destroyed, and your ship will sink.
So my dear friends, ignore the negative triggers from the people around you.
JUST KEEP ON.
Don't look down - you are scaling your own Mt Everest. If you look down, you will descend into an abyss.
Our lives are filled with struggles every day. We need to concentrate on things that are in our control and forget about those that are out of our control.

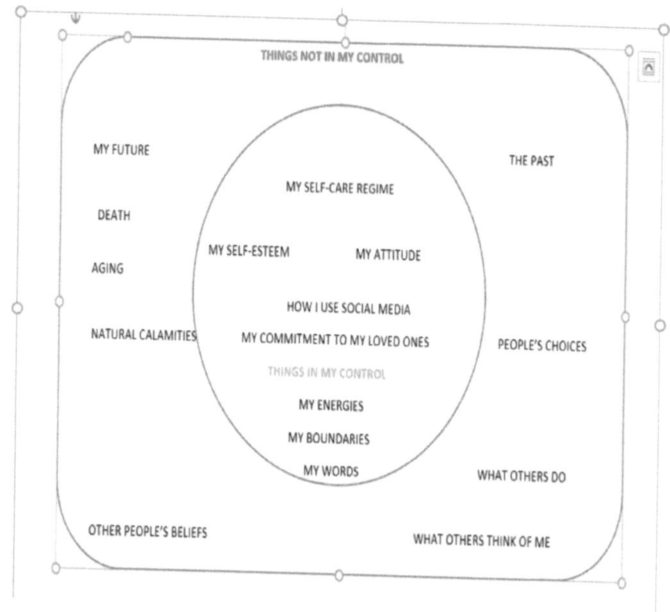

WE NEED TO CONCENTRATE ON THINGS THAT ARE IN OUR CONTROL AND NOT THOSE THAT ARE OUT OF OUR CONTROL.

CHAPTER FIVE

WHEN YOU TRY TO PLEASE ALL, YOU END UP PLEASING NONE.

Do you realize that you can't please all people all the time?

I am sure the following is relevant to you.

WHEN YOU BUY A BLUE CAR

People will say you should have bought the red one.

WHEN YOU START A BUSINESS

They will wonder why you didn't apply for a job.

WHEN YOU ARE NOT GETTING MARRIED

They will say aren't you able to find a suitable match?

WHEN YOU DECIDE TO DO YOUR MASTER IN ECONOMICS

Why didn't you do an MBA?

SO AT THE END OF THE DAY WHEN YOU TRY TO PLEASE ALL, YOU WILL END UP PLEASING NONE. EVERYONE HAS A DIFFERENT OPINION ON EVERYTHING, ABOUT EVERYTHING.

It is not always necessary that it is in agreement with yours. So don't let people bother you.

Only the opinions of those who are close to you should matter to you.
FORGET ABOUT THE REST.
So what should one do—JUST CHILLAX and be less stressed contemplating what others will think of you?
The crux of the matter is that one can't please everyone all of the time.

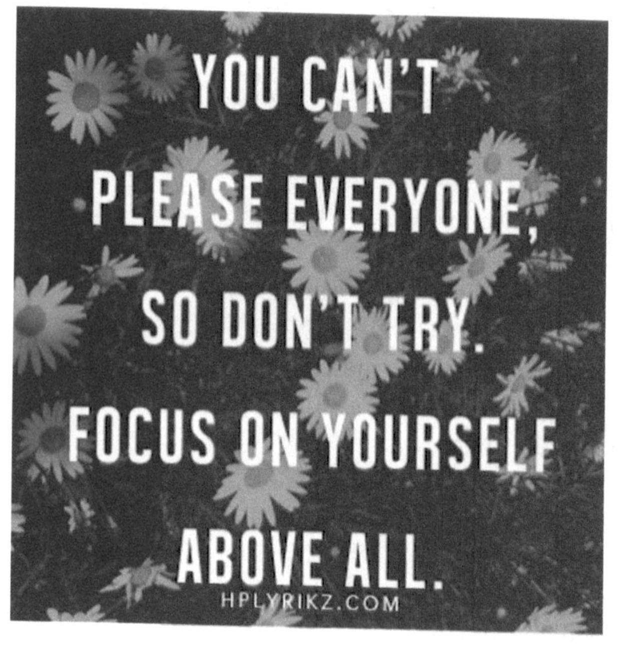

YOU CAN'T PLEASE ALL THE PEOPLE ALL THE TIME.

CHAPTER SIX

BEFORE ENLIGHTENMENT-CHOP WOOD, CARRY WATER;AFTER ENLIGHTENMENT-CHOP WOOD, CARRY WATER

> Before enlightenment;
> chop wood, carry water.
>
> After enlightenment;
> chop wood, carry water.
>
> ZEN KŌAN

A VERY FAMOUS ZEN BUDDHIST PROVERB

Chop wood, carry water is a very famous Zen Buddhist proverb, which can be interpreted in different ways.

For some, it would mean that whether we like it or not, we cannot avoid performing daily prosaic tasks. These may involve performing daily chores, fending for our family, meeting all their needs, and working hard to make ends meet. But ultimately even these daily tasks help us to develop consistency and discipline.

For some others, it would mean that sometimes we chop wood and carry water mindlessly. After we chop the wood and carry the cut wood blocks or put the pitcher of water on our heads and reach our destination, someone was to ask us

'Did you notice that red flower next to the tree whose wood you were chopping?' or

'Did you see the bluebird that sat at the water's edge?'

We are bound to look at that person in an expressionless manner because we did not see anything. Chopping the wood and fetching water were the only monotonous tasks we performed. But what one needs to understand is that the simple technique of chopping wood and transporting water can help us to wire our brains to accomplish strenuous tasks.

Before Enlightenment, it was Chop Wood, Carry Water, and after Enlightenment, it is Chop Wood, Carry Water.

Then what is the dissimilarity?

The difference is in one's interpretation, one's disposition, and one's thinking.

Before becoming spiritually aware, a person was only doing mundane chores like chopping wood and fetching water- without which he would not be able to cook.

But after a spiritual rousing, he is still performing the same tasks— chopping wood, obtaining water- but now he is performing these tasks not casually or carelessly but mindfully.

Since one already knows that it is one's karma to rake wood or fetch water, as no one else can perform these chores for him or her, why can't one do them delightfully instead?

What this means is that if one has to cut wood every day, why not change the axe after a few days? Why not brighten up the axe handle, make it look attractive, or use different pitchers, pots, or vessels for collecting water?

Variety will add spice to the whole act of cutting wood and fetching water. The work will no longer be tedious. At the end of the day, we are ultimately responsible for our own lives. We can at least take control of the reins of life.

We take charge of our finances, of our house but ALLOW someone else to take charge of our lives.

We let ourselves cut wood from nearby trees. We don't dare venture deeper into the woods to explore different species of wood to cut.

Why can't we sing to ourselves every day when we go out to fetch water?

Why don't we allow ourselves to enjoy the music of the brook before filling up our pitchers?

Another factor that we need to take into account is----

'IS THE WOOD CHOPPING US AND THE WATER CARRYING US?'

'OR ARE WE CHOPPING THE WOOD AND CARRYING THE WATER?'

Even the smallest of things should be done most effectively. Although the smallest things may seem difficult at first, with practice and patience, things will become easier.

One should be grateful for the chances that life offers to us, for the opportunity for beginning afresh, and for creating and working for the life that we aspire for.

One should remain committed to oneself and find happiness and peace in each given moment.

LIFE IS TOO SHORT TO HOLD GRUDGES AGAINST PEOPLE. HOLDING ON TO GRUDGES AND NEGATIVE FEELINGS IS A WASTE OF HAPPINESS.

CHAPTER SEVEN

YOU ARE UNIQUE- THE ONLY ONE OF YOUR OWN KIND.

TAKE PRIDE IN BEING YOUR ORIGINAL SELF. DON'T TRY TO BE SOMEONE ELSE'S PHOTOCOPY.

God's factory is the only factory that produces only one piece of its kind. No two people on this earth have the same fingerprints. The chances of two people having the same fingerprints are one in 64 billion. No two fingerprints have ever been confirmed to be identical.

Each finger is likewise unique. So treat yourself as someone special. Love yourself. Don't degrade yourself.

LOOKING GORGEOUS AND FEELING POSITIVE GO TOGETHER.

Wearing stylish clothes, wearing your hair, and taking care of your physical appearance will contribute a long way to boosting your morale, affecting how you feel inside.

We don't always have to do things to please others, but once in a while, we need to step out of our way to please ourselves.

Remember one more thing—WORDS HAVE ENERGY, THEY HAVE POWER.

WE SHOULD NOT SPEAK ANYTHING NEGATIVE ABOUT OURSELVES, EVEN JOKINGLY, BECAUSE WORDS DO NOT KNOW THE DIFFERENCE.

Some very easy stress busters to help you stay fit.

1) listen/play music yourself.

2) Sometimes nutritious food reduces stress, so eat vitamins, Omega 3, almonds, and a rainbow diet.

Have buttermilk every day and avoid coffee as it can mess up your sleep.

3) Avoid spending too much time on SOCIAL MEDIA, and don't keep the phone very close to your face/eyes. It makes anxiety unbearable and even disturbs sleep patterns.

Reduce the time you spend on social media/download apps that help you track the time you spend.

4) Put your phone/laptop in night shift mode to help you sleep better.

5) You can read a few pages of any worthwhile book before sleeping and getting at least 7/8 hrs of sleep is a MUST.

6) Exercise helps reduce stress. You will benefit from exercising/jogging wherever you are sitting and studying. It will provide you with a break a break from studying and working.

7) Playing video games can help one reduce anxiety. They keep one's mind off other things.

IF ANY NEGATIVE THOUGHT OF HARMING YOURSELF IS CONTEMPLATED, JUST GIVE A THOUGHT TO WHAT REPERCUSSIONS IT WILL HAVE ON YOUR NEAR AND DEAR ONES.

CHAPTER EIGHT

LIFE IS NOT A RACE TO THE FINISH. IT IS A JOURNEY TO BE ENJOYED.

If you're having a rough day, select a tip you've never tried before and give it a go. If you want to pay attention to your mental health, you might include an additional ritual in your daily routine.

Remind yourself that it is worthwhile to take a break from your ambitions, desires, aspirations, and intentions-call it whatever you like. In times of quandary/dilemma/cataclysm, it's always a wise idea to relieve as much stress as possible.

Doing so isn't easy. However, the reality of the matter is that life changes, our circumstances change, and we evolve as a result. Sometimes, the plans we had or the goals we planned to reach must be altered too. If you've been seeking someone to tell you that it's acceptable to put a pause on that nonessential activity you said you'd do—well, it surely is.

UNLOAD YOURSELF, AND DECOMPRESS WHAT IS GOING ON INSIDE YOU.

Competition is good but at times it can be strenuous and might lead to undesired outcomes. Comparisons and competitions should be avoided as they can ruin your value.

It is not always necessary that the hares win. A tortoise can also have its day.

I am sure all of you are aware of the end of the story—THE HARE AND THE TORTOISE. After all the tortoise had won in the end. It had not hurried but managed to walk in its own customary leisurely, lazy walk and still managed to win.

REMEMBER YOU ARE WHO YOU ARE AND AT THE END OF THE DAY YOU ARE IRREPLACEABLE—NOT TO YOUR HIGH—UPS, NOT TO YOUR BOSS—BUT TO THOSE TO WHOM YOU MATTER.

LIFE IS NOT A RACE TO THE FINISH

LIFE IS NOT A RACE TO THE FINISH

THE GRASS IS NOT GREENER ON THE OTHER SIDE BUT IS GREENER ON THE SIDE THAT YOU WATER

We are often dazzled by looking at others. It may be due to their job, their elegant house, or their well-settled and qualified children. We generally evaluate a book or novel by its outward appearance. We find the grass greener on the other side of the hedge.

But that is not true.

When we see green grass, we usually want to cross over the hedge to find it.

But once we reach the other side of the hedge, we say to ourselves—LOL, I CAME HERE FOR THIS?

It was only an illusion that the grass was green.

My side wasn't as disastrous as it could have been. So dear noble souls, the grass is not green on the other side, but on the side, that is well-watered and well-tended.

Why are we not able to see the diligent work, the spirit that has been put into the end product—a well-kept house, well-set children, one enjoying the amenities of life?

Had we worked as hard as he did, maybe we too would have been rewarded by all that the person on the other side of the hedge is savoring.

So many students and young professionals want to go abroad. But little do they realize that it is not a piece of cake. Uprooting oneself and starting afresh is not all that easy. Life is different and difficult for immigrants.

If one can work hard in another country, why not here?

Yes, things are better there. More civic sense, less crime, less pollution, fresh air, a well-paid job, good health facilities, etc. But one doesn't have the family, the social bonding that one had back home, the aromas emanating from nearby kitchens, or the commonness of religious celebrations.

But why can't we be the change that we want to see/ inspire in others? Someone has to start watering the grass on this side of the hedge also.

So let us not leave our pastures for the greener ones, but start working on making our pastures also green.

Working hard is all that matters at the end of the day—whether it is on this side of the quickset or the other. Mirages cannot be taken for reality.

CHAPTER TEN

RIVERS AS METAPHORS

LESSONS THAT RIVERS CAN TEACH US.

We are all aware of metaphors—they are figures of speech in which one term or phrase representing one type of thing or thought is substituted for another to convey a similarity or parallel between them.

Nature has so much to teach us.

We have a lot to learn from the life of a river.

Every river has tremendous intrinsic power, rivers being metaphors for the manifestation of life itself

Every person is blessed with it, regardless of how small or imposing they are.

The river begins at the source and ends at the source unerringly.

Flowing gently, vibrantly, caressingly.

The source of the river is the beginning of life depiction

In the course of the river, we meet the sea, symbolizing the end of our convictions in life.

The freshwater ecosystems depend upon the connectivity of rivers

In the eyes of people and animals, they are life-givers.

Species living near rivers can thrive if rivers are healthy

Throughout history, rivers have sustained civilizations upon civilizations in stealth.

The river itself is the personification of life.

Enabling agrestic economies to lead a life without strife.

Rivers sustain ways of life, cultural beliefs, and values

Even festivals used to take place on the Tigris River in the month of Tammuz.

Rivers depict that the powers and energies inside us can be channeled into doing useful and rewarding things

We can thereby derive meaning from our lives by conquering the challenges that life brings.

People can transpose their flows as rivers do.

They transform into something radically different through metamorphosis.

Different states of the river are like different seasons in our life cycle

Learn the lessons of survival. Allow the river to make you its disciple

Don't miss out and explore Mother Nature. Find a lake, a small stream, a river, or a sea.

When you sit on the ground and look at the water's surface, you will find the serenity that you never expected.

Explain to your children that the river forms a border between the underworld and the world of the living.

Rivers connect us. We are thankful to them and so let us not forget them in our prayers of thanksgiving.

"I would love to live like a river flows, carried by the surprise of its unfolding."
John O'Donohue

CHAPTER ELEVEN

WE ARE LISTLESS AT TIMES BECAUSE WE ARE LISTLESS

Sounds odd? Does it? Hahahaha

(FIRST LISTLESS MEANS WITHOUT ENERGY, TIRED, AND THE SECOND LISTLESS MEANS WITHOUT A LIST)

Yes, using lists to reduce stress may seem somewhat vague and out of date, but lists may be one of our better time-management tools.

Making a list might help one calm down. The major issue with today's work is that it never seems to be finished or even accomplished. There's a vast list of activities to complete that one needs to perform. This includes even those minor open loops such as unopened emails, unfinished books to read, and commitments to follow up. All of these factors might cause subconscious tension. And the brain frantically attempts to keep up, but malfunctions several times.

Furthermore, most of the stress stems from striving to keep up with everything, rather than from having a great deal on one's plate. This is why, if we're experiencing consternation, we should sit down, grab a pen, and write a list. We will feel immediate relief after doing this easy activity, even if everything we have mentioned remains incomplete.

Making a list restores one's sense of control. Crossing things off the list can be a rewarding experience. It helps one feel like one has done something, giving one more gratification. Furthermore, one does not have to keep track of the tasks that have been completed. When we cross something off our list, it's done and out of our thoughts.

Our brain's memory functions are improved by making a list. Making a list of activities to perform is an effective way to take notes while listening to a lecture.

MAINTAIN A LIST AND AVOID TENSIONS

STRENGTHEN YOUR FAMILIAL AND SOCIAL TIES, STILL WHEN THERE IS TIME.

Humans are sociable beings who live on connection.

Studies on aging have found that close-knit families and happy marriages lead to improved health and a longer life.

Until now, if you haven't spent quality time with your family(whether it is your own family or the family that you have married into), start doing so now.

Maintain meaningful relationships with your family members regularly.

Quality of time, not the amount of time, is required for meaningful interactions.

Maintain simplicity and engage with your child/elderly parents in ways that are appropriate for your lifestyle and relationship.

Each connection that you make with your kids has a long-term influence and gives your kid the support and comfort he or she requires.

Balancing the demands of the entire family's school, sports, hobbies, and occupations leaves little leisure time. However, maintaining family values may be easier than you think if you are committed to carving out memorable times to share.

Devote time to your elderly parents, and make them feel wanted and cared for.

By showing that you care about the well-being of your family members, they will want to express their difficulties and problems to parents and children, resulting in mutual respect.

Disconnect from the digital world, at least when you are with your family. In today's technologically advanced society, it is common for families to be there but not involved. When you create a technology-free zone, you remove distractions, allowing you to focus on each other.

Set aside time each week to spend with your family without watching television, tablets, laptops, or phones.

MAKE IT A POINT TO BE MINDFULLY PRESENT FOR YOUR FAMILY.

CHAPTER THIRTEEN

WRITE AN EMAIL TO YOURSELF.

We—HOMOSAPIENS, are social animals and cannot live in a vacuum. As human beings, we need to communicate our thoughts, and our feelings to others.

But in today's materialistic world, everyone is busy with their own stressful, disquieting, distressing lives. No one here has the time or even the inclination to care for each other.

There are times when we are annoyed, perturbed, aggravated, or exasperated by people, things, and the environment around us.

We want to communicate/share our apprehensions, worries, and anxieties with the people around us. Sometimes we do and sometimes we are not able to articulate them. When we have revealed them, we regret having done so.

We need to vent out our feelings because if we don't do so, we might be queasy, and jumpy all the time.

So the best person to whom you can talk, to liaise is YOU, YOURSELF.

The best thing to do is to write a mail to yourself, an angry one if you are counseling yourself or admonishing/ reprimanding/ scolding/rebuking yourself.

Write everything that you would be wanting to tell others. Mail this to yourself.

Open the mail, and read it carefully, once, twice, or three times.

THEN DELETE IT.

WRITE AN EMAIL TO YOURSELF, READ IT, AND DELETE IT.

CHAPTER FOURTEEN

SWITCH YOUR MIND TO 'AIRPLANE MODE' NOW AND THEN.

AIRPLANE MODE WILL WORK FOR THE BRAIN AND THE MIND JUST AS WELL, AS IT DOES WITH CELL PHONES AND LAPTOPS.

It can be challenging to switch off in a world where we are constantly 'on.' This is heightened by the accessibility of plentiful electronic devices and Social Media Sites that can distract us both inside and outside of the workplace/home.

Our thinking brain, on the other hand, has limited capacity and requires some rest. Once our mind is calm and relaxed, it can then be at its peak for longer periods.

In reality, we cannot turn off our brains. We would be dead if we did so because it keeps our bodies running. So, how do we soothe our minds and achieve a state of relaxation while remaining alert?

THE ANSWER IS FLIGHT MODE!

THE ADVANTAGES OF PUTTING OUR PHONES/ LAPTOPS ON AIRPLANE MODE

What I didn't realize until I was writing this article was that there are benefits to using airplane mode. This is true no matter whether we're not in the air or on a plane!

They are as follows:

1) DISTRACTIONS CAN BE AVOIDED.— When you know you'll need some alone time or want to avoid some intrusions, switch to airplane mode. This way you know you would get some quiet time and it will keep distractions at bay.

You'll still be able to check your files and time, but you won't be prompted to pick up the phone to check for messages. This is because you won't be getting them!

2) YOU CAN EXTEND THE LIFE OF YOUR BATTERY.—When you've forgotten your charger, set your phone to airplane mode. It enables you to read files, check the time, and take photos while drastically reducing background work. When you need to make a phone call, you can turn off airplane mode.

3) YOU CAN ACCELERATE CHARGING. —When you only have a few minutes and need to charge your phone, turning on airplane mode will expedite the process.

NOW, WHAT HOLDS GOOD FOR OUR MOBILES AND LAPTOPS IS EFFECTIVE FOR OUR BRAINS AND MINDS TOO.

YES, OUR BRAINS AND MINDS TOO CAN BE PUT IN AIRPLANE MODE.

SOME WAYS OF TRANSFORMING OUR BRAINS INTO AN AIRPLANE MODE

Taking some time during the day to turn off some of our transmissions would aid in more effectively utilizing our brain batteries.

Our capacity to work will be enhanced once our brain is rested and out of Airplane Mode. We will be able to do justice to whatever we are doing.

ONE CAN PUT ONE'S BRAIN INTO AIRPLANE MODE IN THE FOLLOWING STEPS:

You can do them all while sitting at your desk, going for a walk, taking a cab/metro, or driving.

1) Breathing consciously

If you're not used to doing this, start with a few minutes and gradually increase your time. Take note of how you're exhaling.

BREATHE IN, BREATHE OUT

BREATHE IN, BREATHE OUT

The inhale, exhale, and space in between —If you concentrate on this, you will notice that it calms your entire body and relaxes your mind.

YOU WILL FEEL BETTER

2) Stay away from distractions, obstructions, intrusions, and diversions—call them whatever you can.

If you need 10 minutes of silence, turn off your phone, close the door, and stop any interruptions/disturbances. DO JUST AND JUST NOTHING.

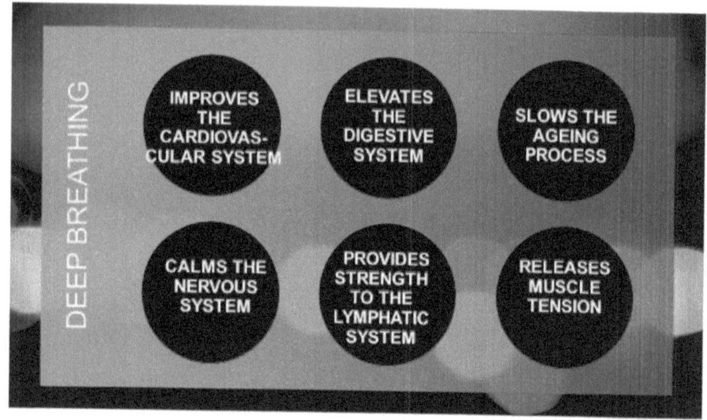

DEEP BREATH

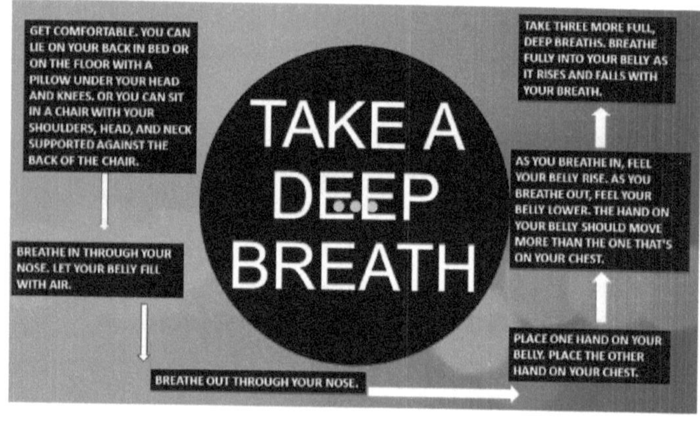

DEEP BREATH

CHAPTER FIFTEEN

BE PENNY-WISE, PAY YOURSELF FIRST

You all must be aware of the recessions around the world, the layoffs, and the financial crunch all around.

We spend money on necessities, desires, and pleasures. When we arrange our money, we can keep track of our costs. Even if we overspend in one month, we will know how much to cut down on in the subsequent months to stay within our budget. This will assist us in determining our revenue requirements, and we will be able to adjust our earning capacity accordingly.

Spending patterns shift as people's lifestyles and stages of life change.

SO AT THE END OF THE DAY, DEAR FRIENDS, MONEY PLAYS A VERY MIGHTY ROLE IN OUR LIVES.

This is especially true as we grow older. Understand your relationship with your hard-earned money. Small details, attention, and gradual improvements, if stressed daily, will come a long way toward assisting us in saving money.

Our goal in today's world should be to modify our negative financial habits. However, this will be challenging because spending habits are ingrained in our daily routines and it may be difficult to distance ourselves from buying sprees. Physically giving up cash rather than mindlessly swiping our card will unquestionably make us more aware of our expenditure and thereby make it easier to track it.

Yet another way of curbing overspending is by taking out a fixed amount of money for the week and spending just what we have.

One can also keep a list of reminders in one's wallet. A marvelous idea is affixing a sticker to one's credit card that reads, "Do you need this?"

Anything and everything that makes you pause before making a purchase might help you make better and wiser decisions.

Unsubscribe or unfollow if you discover that you spend a lot of money after clicking on a marketing email. (You may also be seeing photographs of an Instagram influencer wearing a specific brand, for example).Alternatively, if you buy clothing or makeup when you have time to kill, consider doing something else instead, such as going for a stroll in the park.

THE ESSENTIAL THING YOU SHOULD KEEP IN FOCUS ON IS TO PAY YOURSELF FIRST

"Pay yourself first," a common investor mindset and term in personal finance and retirement-planning literature, refers to automatically routing a preset savings contribution from each paycheck at the time it is received.

Because the savings contributions are automatically routed from each paycheck to your savings or investment account, you are "paying yourself first." So one should pay oneself first, before meeting one's monthly rent and bills, other expenses, or making discretionary purchases.

CHAPTER SIXTEEN

ONE CAN BE HAPPY SIMPLY BY USING ONE'S IMAGINATION

Yes, while you are reading this, it might appear unusual to you, but it is true.

Just by imagining that one is happy, one can attain happiness.

Let us understand how.

Have you ever imagined that everything that has been created in this world, a car, a smartphone, an airplane, or rather all the consumerist items in this world have all been made through one's ideation? The first thing people do when they need something is to visualize it in their minds.

For example, if someone who would have invented the car or the one who would have gotten the idea of the car first—he would have thought about it first in his mind, he would have first considered how a vehicle with four wheels would look that would transport him, then after thinking about it, he would have drawn it. Only after having a clear perception in his mind about what he wanted, what objective it would provide, and how it would look, he would have collected all the existing materials around him to make a rough design of the car.

It is perplexing to think that so many thinkers, scientists, and researchers have created remarkable things only by using their imagination.

Take the example of cooking. Every day one cooks dishes using the basic ingredients but if we imagine in our minds that by adding our flavors, by adding some different spices or some different ingredients, we can make the dish more appealing, then we have done that too by imagining first or by creating that thought in our minds.

Our thoughts vibrate at a higher frequency than the material world. But we can't see them with the human eye. Science has proved that the brain generates waves and frequencies like a radio or antenna.

Our brain produces Delta waves in its deepest stage of sleep when we are not conscious The brain produces Gamma brain waves which vibrate at the highest frequencies and are produced when we are highly conscious. These help us to feel the emotions of happiness, compassion, and love.

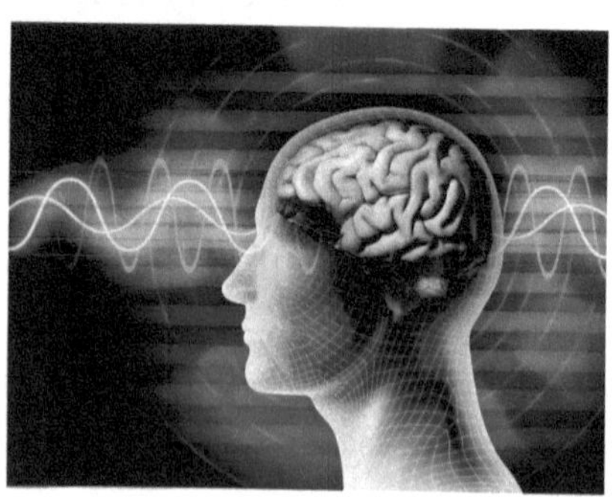

THE PEOPLE WHO MEDITATE, THEIR BRAIN
PRODUCES GAMMA WAVES EASILY.

Meditation has been shown to produce gamma waves in people's brains. When we are awake, in our daily lives, our brain produces delta waves. So it becomes clear that the more conscious we are, the more aware we are the more spiritual growth we have, and the happier we become. Our conceptions can influence our health. Every single thought creates emotions and chemical compounds in our bodies. Just a single thought can make us overtaxed, fearful, anxious, excited, joyful, and content. The more conscious we are, the more we become aware of our thoughts, and we can control and change them. So we can change our mood and health simply by changing our thoughts. When our thoughts are not positive for ourselves or others, they have low frequencies, which fail to create any positive emotion. The brighter our thoughts, the brighter our emotions

POSITIVE EMOTIONS ARE ADVANTAGEOUS FOR OUR RATIONALE, WHILE NEGATIVE EMOTIONS ARE A DANGER TO REASON.

PRACTISING BEING HAPPY BY IMAGINING THAT WE ARE HAPPY WITH SIMPLE EXERCISES.

1) IMAGINING OUR HAPPY FACE

It is time to feel like a child again.

Sit comfortably, close your eyes, and picture yourself, think of your face—if that is difficult, then look at a photo of yours in which you were joyful, think of your glowing face. Visualize your face as if you were smiling, with the brightest smile that you have ever had. When you imagine yourself like this you feel happy. You don't need any particular reason to smile or to be cheerful, there shouldn't be any reason for you to be cheerful, YOU DESERVE TO BE JOYOUS. You should be happy because YOU EXIST, you are the greatest creation of God.

When you create the thought of being content, you create it in your mind, and that creates the emotion of happiness.

2) IMAGINE YOU ARE PARTICIPATING WITH BUTTERFLIES, AND ANGLES AROUND YOU.

Try to visualize colors, flowers, and fairies around you.

Imagine yourself dancing with them. Imagine yourself being carefree with them.

3) IMAGINE YOURSELF FLYING ABOVE THE MOUNTAINS OR SEAS.

Imagine yourself cruising overseas, along rivers, and mountains. Imagine yourself flying above the clouds. Feel the nature around you, feel yourself breathing in the fresh mountain air.

Mountains can conjure up our most primordial emotions and feelings.

Imagine yourself in a world full of colorful lights around you.

Let your imagination be free and enjoy this. As you start imagining these things, your energy will start vibrating at higher frequencies. Let your imagination be free and enjoy this wonderful adventure.

Think about everything and anything that makes you feel happy.

After some practice, you will be able to imagine with your eyes open. You will find it incredible when you will be able to combine this beautiful world that you have created in your mind with your everyday life.

EVERYTHING AROUND YOU WILL APPEAR SO BEAUTIFUL, SO MAGICAL.

The more you practice meditation and imagining techniques, your mental vision will increase and after some time and some practice, you will be able to imagine anything effortlessly.

Even more than meditating, focusing on your breathing will lead to an increase in gamma wave production. Gamma rays support your processing of information.

4) IMAGINE EVERYTHING AROUND YOU EMITS LIGHT.

You will be able to increase your frequencies as well as the frequencies around you just by thinking that everything around you is filled with light.

When you imagine that everything around you emits light, you will be able to transform and change the energies around you.

Imagine the ocean of light that is all around you descending upon you, filling your body. Experience the love and peace of this light

Then slowly imagine that this light is spreading to your house—to all your rooms, then to your locality, then to your country, and then to the whole world.

OUR BRAIN PRODUCES HIGH INTENSITIES OF GAMMA WAVES. THE MORE WE MEDITATE, THE MORE SPIRITUAL WE ARE, THE HIGHER IS OUR TENDENCY OF BEING HAPPIER AND MORE RECEPTIVE.

CHAPTER SEVENTEEN

HOW SHOULD ONE HAVE THEIR VEGGIES--COOKED OR RAW?

The debate about how one should have veggies is not new.

There are differences of opinion about How to Get the Most Out of our Vegetables: Raw or Cooked?

Heat, oil, and cooking time may all impact the nutritional content of a vegetable. Here, we will delve into how to optimize the number of vitamins and minerals that we can get from our veggies.

A healthy diet that includes vitamins is part of many of our daily routines. More than half of us take supplements every week, some of us engage in damaging juice cleanses, and a few of us even receive unneeded vitamin injections. However, it turns out that the secrets to optimizing our nutrition may not be in a bottle (or needle), but rather in the kitchen.

Vegetables are high in vitamins, minerals, antioxidants, and fiber, and the number of nutrients we retain from them is impacted by how they are prepared. Some nutrients are better absorbed from raw veggies, while others are better absorbed from cooked vegetables.

The health advantages of raw vs cooked veggies vary.

While cooked veggies might allow us access to additional nutrients, uncooked vegetables offer more fiber, help maintain healthy digestion, and decrease cholesterol and moderate blood sugar levels. Furthermore, certain foods provide various vitamins depending on whether they are fresh or boiled. For example, spinach: In its raw form, this leafy green delivers vitamin C, while in its cooked form, it offers more vitamin A.

So we should be prudent in adding an amalgamation of veggies in cooked and raw form to our meals.

Knocked-up vegetables provide more soluble vitamins, minerals, and antioxidants because their fiber or cell walls are broken down, making their contents more accessible.

How about steaming our vegetables?

According to several types of research, cooking methods affect the nutritional content of a vegetable. Some researchers, for example, tested five home-cooking strategies for broccoli.

Stir-frying

Microwaving

And boiling broccoli resulted in lower quantities of chlorophyll, soluble protein, carbohydrates, and vitamin C. Broccoli steamed did not have the same impact.

This was because some cooking methods allow water-soluble nutrients (such as vitamins C, B, and D) to leach out, resulting in lower nutritional levels.

Overall, steaming has been demonstrated to be a pretty reliable cooking method.

Steaming is still frequently chosen due to its ability to

maintain the moisture content and nutritional value of vegetables.

Make an effort to cook quickly.

According to researchers, the reason stir-frying vegetables decreases nutrients may be related to the duration of cooking time. The secret to cooking vegetables efficiently is to allow the minerals and vitamins to escape. Roasting, barbecuing, or grilling veggies are effective options because they prepare in the shortest amount of time. Steaming and pan-frying are other nutritious alternatives.

When veggies are covered with a lid, minerals, and vitamins are preserved. But what needs to be kept in mind is that boiling vegetables at high temperatures might alter the nutritional makeup of vegetables.

Raw foods are not appropriate for everyone. Some raw veggies may be difficult for some people to handle, particularly those with gastrointestinal difficulties. Cruciferous vegetables, such as cabbage, broccoli, and cauliflower, are high in nutrients both fresh and cooked. They contain a lot of antioxidants and a lot of vitamin C. However, certain veggies are more prone to producing gas or bloating. It is recommended that you eat cruciferous vegetables soft and prepared to avoid gastrointestinal problems.

Is there a reason why we shouldn't air-cook our vegetables? Air-fried foods are discerned as an excellent substitute for deep-cooked foods because less oil is required, and air-fried meals are perceived as a healthier, lower-fat replacement for deep-fried dishes. Air fryers work by using pressurized heat, and the temperature lowers nutrients. Regular consumption of air-fried foods may increase the risk of certain types of cancer. But that doesn't mean that one should never use an air fryer; rather, use it as a last resort.

Combine veggies and healthy fats.

Healthy fats can improve a vegetable's nutritional value. Olive oil and avocado have phenols, which are antioxidants, so when you combine them with vegetables (for example leafy greens), they absorb those antioxidants, increasing the variety of nutrients. It's also vital to evaluate the number of high-quality fats in the oil and the smoke point of the oil.

Make nutritious vegetable soups—and sample the broth!

Because soups are often made by simmering vegetables in broth on the stove, it's reasonable to expect vitamins and minerals to leach out. But no worries, we'll end up drinking the liquids the meals are in, so we'll get them back.

One should not rely on vegetable juice.

Juicing veggies and fruits is not good because juicing them reduces their nutritional and vitamin content. Therefore eating whole fruits and vegetables is recommended. When we juice, we lose a lot of the fiber and nutrients that are in the skins of these fruits.

A smoothie filled with whole vegetables might be an excellent option.

PROMISE TO TRY TO EAT OUR FRUIT AND VEGETABLES AS WELL AS POSSIBLE AND NOT DRINK THEM.

DISCLAIMER

How one chooses to eat fruits and vegetables differs from person to person.

These are only suggestions from my side. (from my readings, discussions, and some research). I'm not an expert on the subject.

CHAPTER EIGHTEEN

A TOXIC BOMB IS TICK, TICK, TICKING

A DANGEROUS (TOXIC) BOMB IS TICKING

Toxic overload is a state of affairs in which the body contains an uncontrolled amount of toxins. These minacious compounds are found in water, food, cleaning products, and other environmental sources, and many people are persistently exposed to them.

• Given the variety of toxins that could enter your body from the food you eat, such as additives, preservatives, and food contamination, as well as the air pollutants in the air, toxic overload could be a serious health risk.

• Toxins are also created in the body as a consequence of poor gut health, a process known as autotoxicosis.

• Toxic Overload Warning Signs to Look Out For.

• IF YOU ARE FACING SOME/MANY OF THE FOLLOWING Symptoms, IT MEANS THAT TOXINS ARE BUILDING UP INSIDE YOUR BODY

• Feeling sluggish/inactive or tired all the time/Fatigue

• Bloating and poor digestive health

• Constipation or irregular bowel movements

(Or in other words, if you need something like a mobile, a newspaper in the washroom for quite some time)

• you have trouble focusing/ Brain fog
• problems sleeping
• mood changes
• Weight gain
• Dark circles under the eyes.

If you are facing many of these issues or a majority of them, then you need to consider making some lifestyle adjustments. These include eating a nutritious diet and going through detoxification procedures. Managing toxic overload can be significantly simplified with these.

TODAY WE DON'T HAVE THE TIME AND INTENTION FOR OUR HEALTH AND WELLNESS.
TOMORROW, WE WILL HAVE TO DEVOTE MORE TIME AND MONEY TO OUR ILLNESS.

The causes of all illnesses, as well as their cures, are similar. All diseases have the same root cause, which is the formation of deleterious (toxic) materials in the body, except for trauma and environmental exposures. The removal of morbid material from the body is the fundamental treatment strategy for all diseases. Toxins, the root cause of disease, should be eliminated from the body to treat illnesses.

The most effective healer is nature. The ability to heal is inside the human body itself, allowing it to fend off illness and recover its health if necessary.

We need to remove toxins from our bodies or in other words, the unwanted, unused matter from our bodies requires to be removed. This is if we need to cure our diseases and illnesses.

For one's body to function correctly, one must drink water every day. One loses water during the day and when sleeping due to breathing, sweating, and passing stool through the digestive system.

To stay hydrated at night, some individuals take a glass of water before bed. Yet, many are divided on whether or not drinking water before bedtime is beneficial.

It is critical to monitor one's water consumption since drinking water at the wrong time might cause bloating, inappropriate digestion, and other problems. Drinking water should be avoided at the following times:

Drinking a lot of water while or after eating dilutes the digestive juices, preventing your body from effectively absorbing nutrients.

Avoid gulping water when standing up since it puts a strain on your throat.

Avoid drinking water while standing up since it strains your kidneys. Always consume water when seated.

CHAPTER NINETEEN

WHEN TO HAVE WATER AND WHEN NOT TO HAVE WATER

For one's body to function perfectly, women should drink at least 11.5 cups and men should drink at least 15.5 cups of water daily. However one also loses water every day and when sleeping due to breathing, sweating, and passing stool from the digestive system.

To stay hydrated during the night, some individuals take a glass of water before bed. Yet, many are divided on whether or not drinking water before bedtime is beneficial.

It is critical to monitor one's water consumption since drinking water at the wrong time might cause bloating, inappropriate digestion, and other problems. Drinking water should be avoided at the following times:

- Drinking a lot of water while or after eating dilutes the digestive juices, preventing your body from effectively absorbing nutrients.

- Avoid gulping water when standing up since it puts a strain on your throat.

- Avoid drinking water while standing up since it strains your kidneys. Always consume water when seated.

- Drinking too much water before going to bed might disrupt one's sleep and may lead one to stay awake.

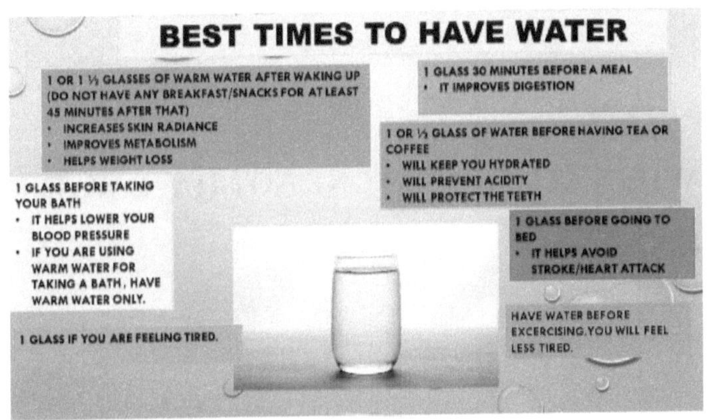

WHEN ALL SHOULD ONE HAVE WATER

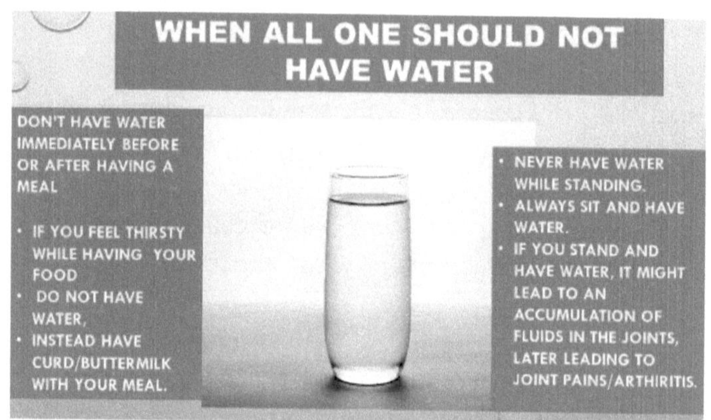

WHEN ALL SHOULD ONE NOT HAVE WATER

CHAPTER TWENTY

EAT THE RAINBOW FOR YOUR HEALTH INCLUDE VIBGYOR IN YOUR DAILY DIET.

EAT THE RAINBOW FOR YOUR HEALTH

We are constantly surrounded by a profusion of fresh fruits and veggies. Markets are bursting with delicious produce, each as dazzlingly colorful as the next. It's like a palpable rainbow in front of our eyes. Simply spectacular!

Remember in your school days – V-I-B-G-Y-O-R? LET US PLAY THAT GAME - BUT NOT WITH COLOURS, BUT THIS TIME WITH FOOD.

We will see what colors we should look for when we shop next for our fruits and vegetables and why.

RED FOODS

Besides their beautiful color, red foods are very high in lycopene which can significantly reduce the risk of cancers like prostate, lung, stomach, and breast. Red foods are also predominantly very high in antioxidants, which have also been found to help prevent cancer and other diseases like

Alzheimer's.

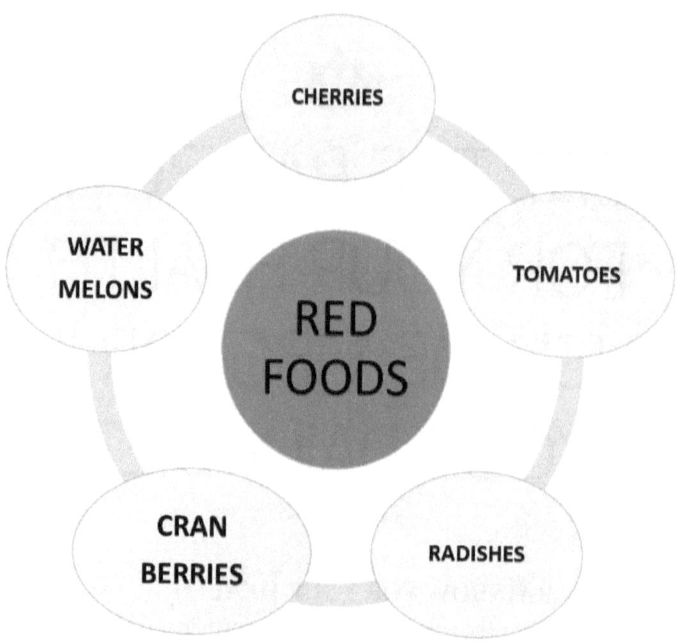

INCLUDING RED FOODS CAN ASSIST REDUCE CANCER RISKS

ORANGE FOODS

Best known for their high levels of beta-carotene, which is extremely beneficial for eye health, orange foods have a world of other health benefits too. Most notably, they are high in vitamins A and C, which are both critical for immune health.

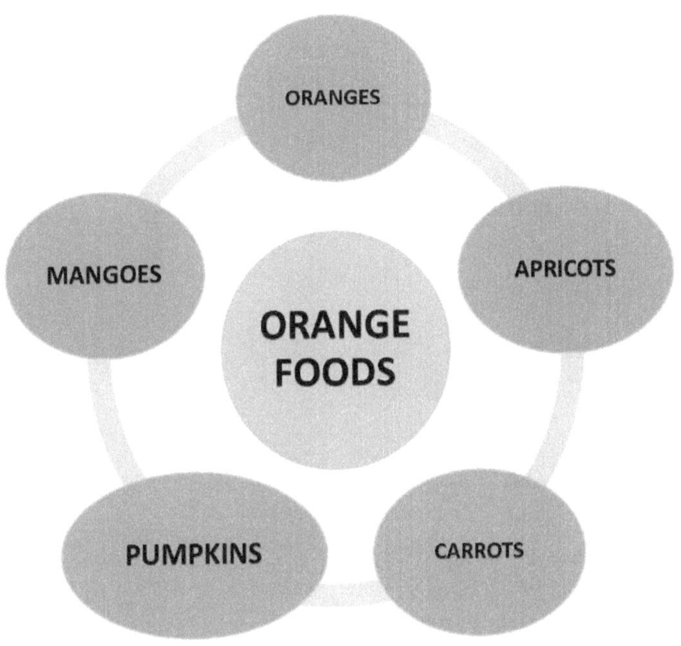

ORANGE FOOD ITEMS IN THE DAILY DIET ARE
RICH IN VITAMINS A & C

YELLOW FOODS

The beauty of the color yellow is the sensation we get when we gaze at it. It enhances our mood and makes us cheerful. But along with its mood-enhancing qualities, and comparable to our orange friends, yellow produce is loaded with vitamin C, which we know helps keep the immune system in tip-top shape.

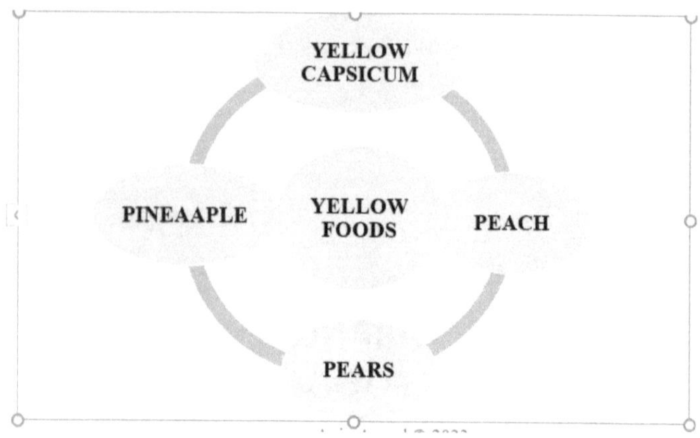

YELLOW FOODS ARE GOOD FOR THE IMMUNE SYSTEM

GREEN FOODS

GREEN IS THE KING, QUEEN, PRINCE, AND PRINCESS OF THE FOOD KINGDOM.

The healthiest and most nutrient-dense foods we can eat are these amazing green foods.

Most notably, leafy fruits and veggies are high in fiber which can be a paramount factor in maintaining a healthy weight and enabling one to live longer.

Green foods are also high in vitamins A, C, and E, all of which are essential daily vitamins. Certain plant-based vegetables include protein, making them ideal for vegetarians and vegans. One should eat something nutrient-dense at all meals, including breakfast!

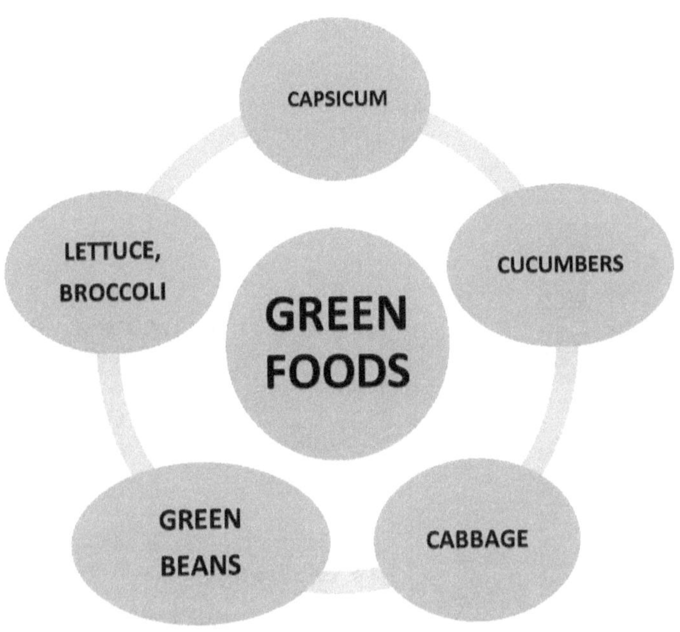

GREEN IS THE KING, QUEEN, PRINCE, AND PRINCESS OF THE FOOD KINGDOM.

BLUE, INDIGO, AND PURPLE FOODS

BLUE FOODS

They include more antioxidants than any other meal, as well as fiber and vitamin C.

INDIGO VIOLET—PURPLE FOODS

Purple foods are nutrient superstars. To start, they're rich in antioxidants. But our purple friends also help avert premature aging, reduce the probability of cancer, and help improve our memory. Plus they're healthy for our hearts (they're packed with flavonoids). Not to mention they're visually appealing.

PURPLE FOODS ARE NUTRIENT SUPERSTARS

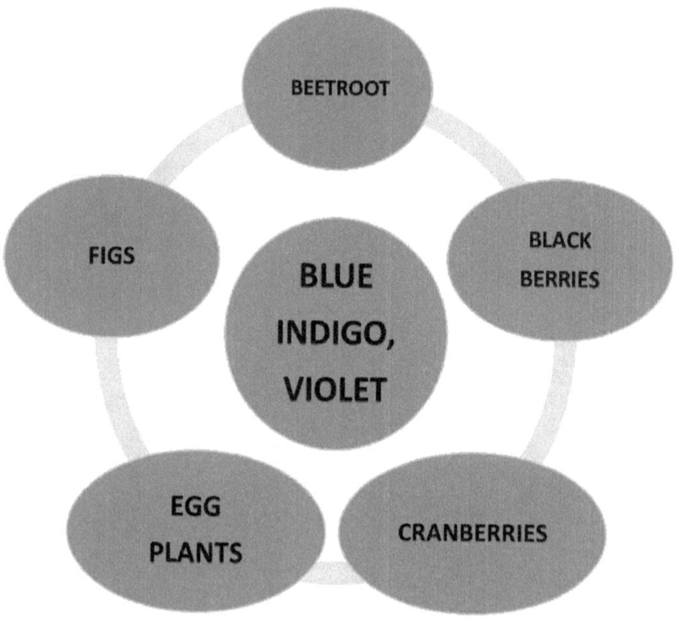

PURPLE FOODS ARE NUTRIENT SUPERSTARS

LET US EAT THE RAINBOW
AND PROVIDE RAINBOW DIETS TO OUR
FAMILY EACH DAY.

CHAPTER TWENTY-ONE

EAT YOUR MEALS MINDFULLY

Mealtime is generally a time of multitasking: we mindlessly chew on chips/popcorn while scrolling through Facebook or devour a dish of pasta/noodles while watching Netflix. Mindful eating is not the in thing these days.

Now one would ask--How is mindful eating differently from simply eating?

Simply put--Mindful Eating is the technique of giving complete attention to the eating experience: identifying hunger and fullness cues, noticing emotions, and observing the scents, flavors, and textures of the meals. When you eat consciously, you automatically slow down, consume less, and have better digestion. Close your laptop, put away your phone, turn off the TV, and devote your whole attention to the food in front of you as the first step in becoming a mindful eater.

Eat till you're satisfied.

Even if we don't stuff ourselves regularly, many of us frequently overeat to the point of discomfort and regret. Our tummies are extremely pliable!

The hassle is that overeating causes weight gain and intestinal issues. Instead, want to feel light and energetic after eating?

So this is what one can do to solve the problem--As one starts each meal, take a moment to measure your physical hunger on a scale of 0 (ravenous) to 10 (overstuffed), and strive to put down your utensils when you reach a 7.

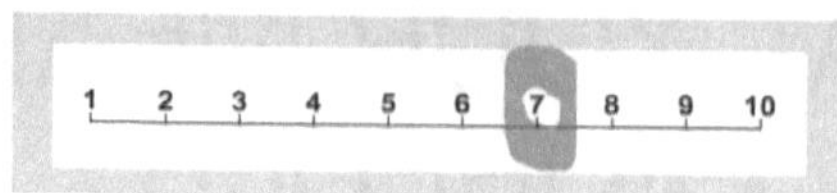

STOP YOURSELF FROM EATING MORE WHEN YOU REACH 7 ON YOUR HUNGER SCALE(OUT OF 10)

At that point, use the following gesture to indicate that you are finished: Cover your plate with a napkin, shove your plate forward, cross your silverware over your plate, or just say "I'm satisfied" out loud.

EAT MINDFULLY

CHAPTER TWENTY-TWO

IKIGAI--THE JAPANESE SECRET OF LONGEVITY

I am excited to discuss the Japanese longevity secret with you.
The secret of 'IKIGAI'.

Ikigai, Japan's equivalent to 'joie de vivre,' is a longevity secret.

The Japanese practice 'Ikigai,' an ancient ideology that teaches that instead of just surviving, one should seek joy and meaning in life.

It is necessary for life satisfaction and finding joy and purpose in many facets of one's life. This includes helping others, eating properly, and being surrounded by loving friends and family.

A happy life is the best existence we can aspire to. It's the type of life that makes us feel satisfied and motivates us to have ambitious expectations for the future. Pure joy may appear to be a transitory experience, yet even if we only feel it for a short period, we are likely to hold onto it. We can enjoy it.

One need not have any special, unique talents that one has to pursue. In addition to enjoying our morning coffee, getting ready for work, getting to work, and reaching our workplace, doing things mindfully and happily are our reasons for living.
One should take pleasure in whatever one is doing.
Every day should be a day to look forward to.

SEEK JOY AND MEANING IN WHATEVER YOU DO.

CHAPTER TWENTY-THREE

TRY A TEA MEDITATION.

INDULGE IN A TEA MEDITATION NOW AND THEN

Life is hectic, and it might be tough to find a few moments to pause and be still to meditate. But mix it with a cup of tea, and peace beckons.....

TRY A TEA MEDITATION

Perhaps in your drawing room, sitting room, kitchen, bedroom, or garden.....

From the time you make room for a tea meditation, become aware of each step: the selection of tea, the pouring of water, and the sensations that transport you from the outside world to the inner realm .....and into a state of clarity and equilibrium.....

As you sip your tea, pay attention to any ideas, emotions, feelings, or sensations that arise. Appreciate them without absorbing or clinging to them, and without passing judgment, before returning your attention to the tea.....

Pay attention to the sensation of being present in a place where there is silence, deep serenity, and a caring sense of being welcomed at this moment....... Allow meditative sessions to conclude naturally.

After you've finished your last sip, gently set the cup down and sit quietly for a few moments.

TAKE OUT YOUR BEST CROCKERY IF YOU WANT
AFTER ALL IF NOT YOU THEN WHO?
LISTEN TO SOME SOFT MUSIC

TAKE OUT YOUR BEST CROCKERY FOR YOUR TEA
MEDITATION

CHAPTER TWENTY-FOUR

WATER STORED IN COPPER VESSELS IS VERY BENEFICIAL FOR HEALTH.

USES OF COPPER WATER

WATER STORED IN COPPER VESSELS IS USEFUL
Dear readers,

Let me share an ancient Indian SECRET WITH YOU.
Here I am aiming to delve into the uses of copper water, how to preserve copper water as well as how to care for your copper vessels.

#Copper is a crucial component of melanin, the natural dark pigment that imparts color to the skin, hair, and eyes.
#Copper is an excellent brain stimulant. It cleanses the kidneys and the gastrointestinal tract.
#The water accumulated in a copper vessel can positively charge the water and has also been shown to help stop seizures

#Copper has anti-inflammatory properties that aid in the healing of rheumatoid arthritis and other inflammatory pains. Enthrallingly, Naturopathy knew this even when pathogens were still unknown to science.

#According to Ayurveda, water should generally be placed in copper vessels.

#Copper vessels were utilized by the ancient Egyptians to keep water fresh. Experts claim that a copper vessel could be the alternative to eliminating the bacterium that causes food poisoning.

Drinking Water Correctly and Safely from a Copper Bottle

#Purchase a pure copper vessel or bottle.

#Fill the bottle with water and store it somewhere cool and dry overnight all day, or for 8 hours. The bottle should not be stored in a refrigerator.

#Dear friends, the best time to consume water stored in a copper bottle is always first thing in the morning on an empty stomach.

#Do not overdo it; drinking water stored in a copper bottle twice a day (morning and evening) is more than enough to provide your body with the recommended amount of copper.

#Take breaks from drinking from a copper bottle.

#Take a month off after drinking water from a copper bottle constantly for two months. This enables the human body to eliminate excess copper.

How to Clean Your Copper Utensils

#Copper will naturally darken over time. The copper oxidizes with water and must be cleaned regularly.

#Rub the utensils with the juice of a lime or even tamarind(tamarind indicia). After a few minutes, use water to rinse the vessels/utensils.

COPPER IS AN EXCELLENT BRAIN STIMULANT. IT CLEANSES THE KIDNEYS AND THE GASTROINTESTINAL TRACT.

COPPER IS AN EXCELLENT BRAIN STIMULANT. IT CLEANSES THE KIDNEYS AND THE GASTROINTESTINAL TRACT.

Disclaimer

The information provided is solely instructive and educational, and should not be interpreted as medical advice.

Please use the content only in consultation with an appropriate certified medical or healthcare professional.

CHAPTER TWENTY-FIVE

FRUITS ARE GOOD FOR HEALTH,BUT THERE IS A TIME TO EAT YOUR FRUITS.

All of us know that fruits can do marvels for our health, but we can't have fruits as and when we like them. Consuming fruits daily is an excellent habit.

But there are some things to keep in mind while having fruits too.

Fruits are high in fiber and vitamins, which are good for our bodies and health. They're also naturally low in sodium, fat, and added sugar.

While all fruits are nutritious, some have compelling scientific evidence to support their health claims. Lemons, blueberries, and apples are some examples, as are oranges, raspberries, pomegranates, and grapefruit.

The fruit has health advantages in several forms, including fresh, frozen, canned, and freeze-dried. Even pure fruit juice has certain health advantages.

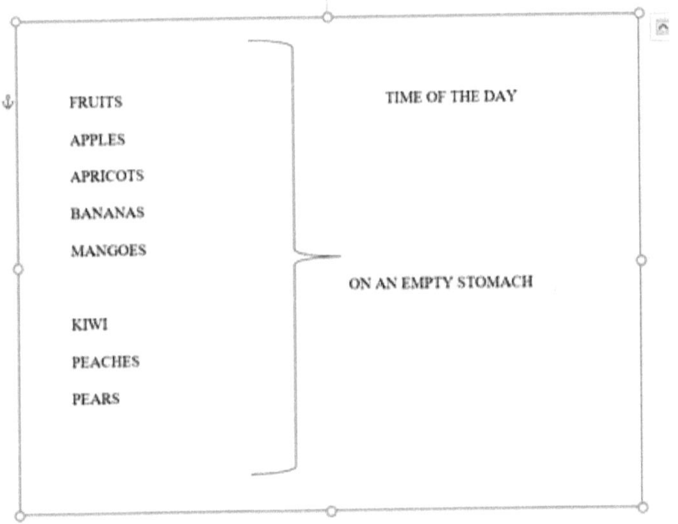

WHICH FRUITS TO HAVE AND WHEN

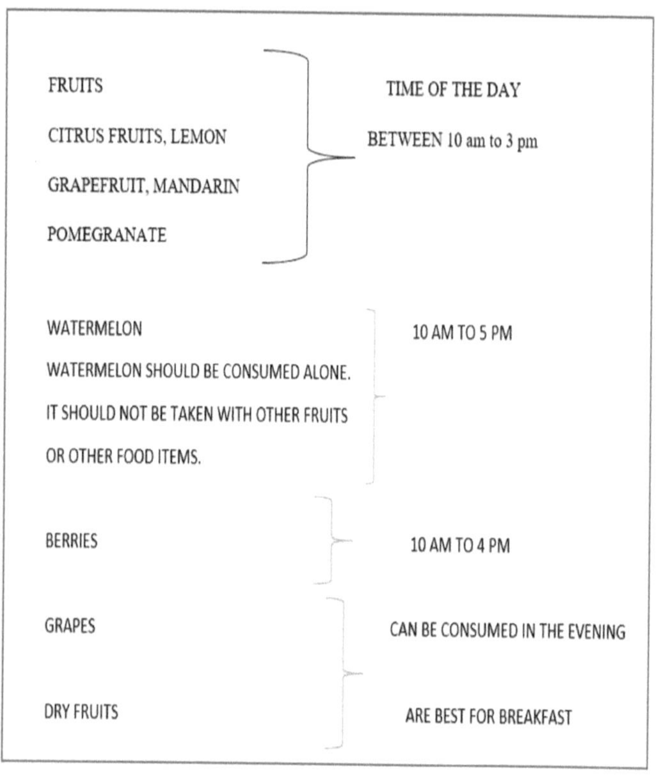

WHICH FRUIT TO HAVE AND WHEN.

AVOID COMBINING FRUITS WITH YOUR MEALS.

AVOID COMBINING FRUITS WITH YOUR MEALS.
• Do not combine fruit with your meal. After your fruit diet, leave a gap for the next meal.
• Don't mix fruit with yogurt.
• Eat each fresh fruit separately.
• Do not store fresh fruit juice for long. Consume the juice Immediately.
• DO NOT DRINK YOUR FRESH FRUITS.

CHAPTER TWENTY-SIX

NOBODY/NOTHING IS USELESS IN THIS WORLD. IT IS HOW WE PERCEIVE THINGS.

NOBODY/NOTHING IS USELESS IN THIS WORLD.
IT IS HOW WE PERCEIVE THINGS.

Once a saint had to travel to the nearby well to draw water for his daily household chores.

For this purpose, he decided to use a stick to which he had attached two buckets. The left side bucket had a tiny hole in it as a result of which water would drop on the way from the well to the saint's house.

This lasted for many months.

One day the right side bucket made fun of the left side bucket. He said, 'You are so useless, and look at me, I am so useful for my master. I brought the whole amount of water to the house and you came back only 1/3 filled dropping and wasting so much on the way.'

The bucket on the left felt very ashamed and started weeping.

The next day when the saint got ready to fetch water, the left side bucket said to him, 'Master why don't you get rid of me? I am of no use to you. Please use a new bucket instead.'

The saint smiled and replied, 'Who says you are useless? You have been doing quite well. Look along the path leading from the well to the house. Greenery abounds on the left side and beautiful flowers bloom everywhere. All this has only been possible because of you. The left side has been receiving tiny drops every day. While on the other hand, there is no greenery on the right side of the path. The flowers that I offer to God every day are the ones that I pluck from the right side of the path. So there is a big contribution from your side also to my worship of God.'

A feeling of joy and usefulness filled the left bucket as the saint spoke.

So we must remember that often helpful deeds are done unknowingly.

Fault or no-fault, every person is unique in itself.

So we should not waste time finding fault in others.

CHAPTER TWENTY-SEVEN

BE A RAINBOW TO YOUR OWN CLOUD

YOU HAVE ALREADY BEEN A RAINBOW TO SO MANY PEOPLE'S CLOUDS

YOU HAVE BEEN A RAINBOW TO SO MANY
PEOPLE'S CLOUDS

YOU HAVE PLAYED SO MANY ROLES
BUT WHAT ABOUT YOU------

.........NOW BE A
RAINBOW TO YOUR CLOUD
FIND TIME FOR YOURSELF
FIND TIME FOR SELF REALISATION
   TAKE OUT TIME FOR SELF-CARE
   REMEMBER SELF CARE DOESN'T MEAN THAT YOU
ARE BEING SELFISH.

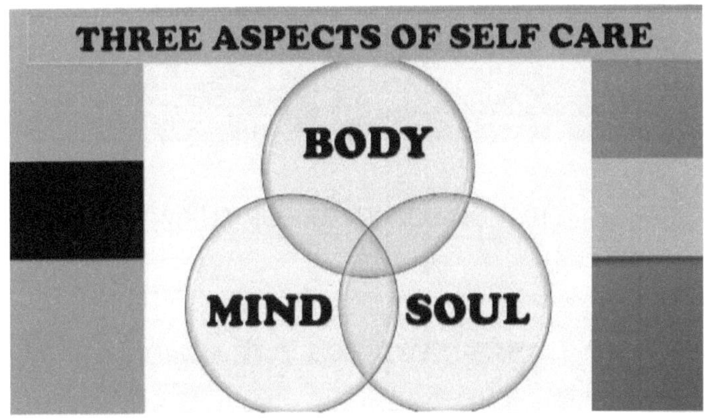

THERE ARE THREE ASPECTS OF SELF-CARE-BODY,
MIND, AND SOUL.

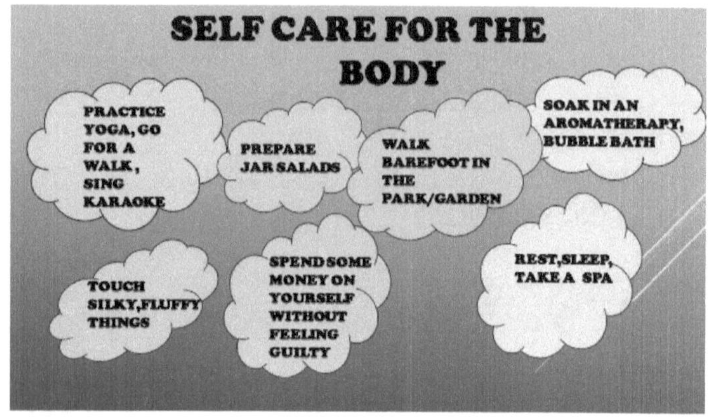

TIPS FOR SELF-CARE FOR THE BODY

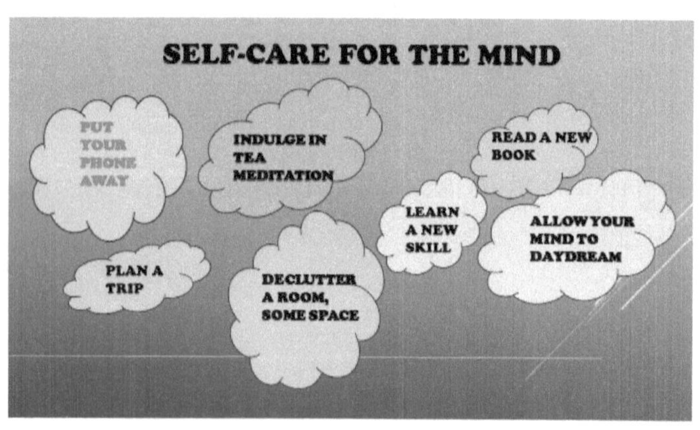

TIPS FOR SELF-CARE FOR THE SOUL

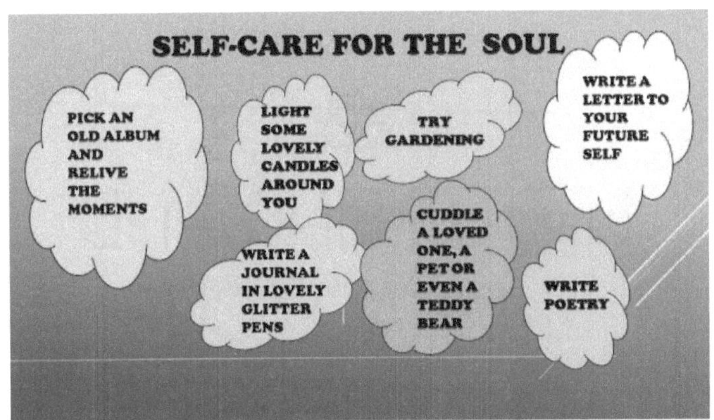

TIPS FOR SELF-CARE FOR THE MIND

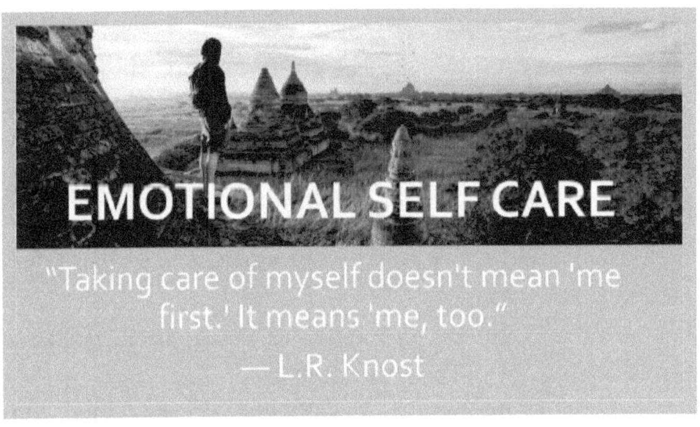

EMOTIONAL SELF-CARE IS NOT TANTAMOUNT TO BEING SELFISH

CHAPTER TWENTY-EIGHT

LET US FIND AND EMBRACE OUR SPRINKLERS OF GLEE.

All of us have endured a lot of traumas in the last two years. Covid has deeply impacted us physically, morally, psychologically, and financially. 2020,2021,2022 were challenging for us.

But let bygones be bygones.

All of us should strive to find our sprinklers of happiness and embrace them.

Let us break our contentment into small, small drops of water oozing out of the sprinklers.

We must make happiness and self—care more manageable.

All of us know that self-care is critical, but help us not to make it so intimidating. Your goal shortly should be to prioritize yourself.

Please allow yourself to take delight in tiny things like buying yourself an elegant dress. We can also make us bake a delicious, lovely cake for ourselves, and go for a walk on a sunny day. Let us not make our self-care regime a time-consuming, infrequent activity.

Consider making our self—care a daily routine like bathing, eating, etc. something extravagant instead of a boring routine.

Let us celebrate ourselves and the small accomplishments that we attain every day.

FIND YOUR SPRINKLERS OF JOY

SEEK HAPPINESS IN SMALL SMALL THINGS

CHAPTER TWENTY-NINE

HAVE WATER SITTING AND MILK STANDING

You will be surprised after reading this--but it is true.

One should always drink water while sitting rather than standing.

Reasons

1)by standing and drinking, you disrupt the body's fluid balance, which may lead to an increase in the accumulation of fluids in the joints, causing arthritis.

2)by sitting and drinking, your muscles and nervous system are relaxed, which allows the nerves to easily digest food and other fluids.

3)while sitting, your kidneys also pace the filtration process.

On the contrary, one should consume milk while sitting down and never while standing.

For a variety of reasons, doctors advise against drinking milk while sitting.

1) while sitting, the milk traverses half of your body at a normal pace. But then it has a speed breaker due to your sitting posture. As a result, transport to the rest of your

body slows.

2) but if you stand, the milk will pass down your body without any obstruction. Your bloodstream will pick it up and rapidly transport it to all parts of your body, absorbing every nutrient that milk has to offer.

ALWAYS SIT AND HAVE WATER.

STACK UP A LOT OF FERMENTED FOODS FOR GOOD HEALTH.

HEALTH BENEFITS OF FERMENTED FOODS.

Fermented foods were an integral component of many cultures' diets, and fermentation has been associated with a variety of health benefits over time. As a consequence, the production process and the subsequently fermented chemicals have increasingly aroused scientific curiosity.

Consuming fermented foods offers several health advantages. Some of the most significant ones include

Improving your immune system

If you add a few servings every week, you will be able to relieve digestion.

Because the health benefits of fermented foods were unknown in the past, humans mostly employed fermentation to preserve goods, increase shelf life, and improve flavor.

Furthermore, microbes that contribute to the fermentation process have recently been linked to several health advantages. Therefore, these microorganisms have become an increasingly popular focus of interest.

Several bioactive peptides have anti-oxidant, anti-microbial, opioid-antagonistic, anti-allergenic, and blood pressure-reducing properties. Fermented foods are therefore anti-oxidant, anti-microbial, anti-fungal, anti-inflammatory, anti-diabetic, and anti-atherosclerotic.

Indians can have dosa, and idli—they are nutritious fermented foods.

SOME FERMENTED FOODS THAT ONE MUST STACK UP MORE AND THEREBY CONSUME MORE

FERMENTED FOOD JARS

PICKLED CUCUMBER

CHAPTER THIRTY-ONE

SQUEEZE IN A WORKOUT/EXERCISE SNACK.

It's difficult to get enough exercise these days. Maybe you used to commute to the gym or ride your bike to work or school, but not anymore. Maybe now you even rarely leave the house.

The world we live in today is less mobile and more constrained.

BUT THERE IS SOMETHING TO CHEER ABOUT.

What are the glad tidings?

TAKE AN EXERCISE SNACK.

With so much time at home, it's simpler than ever to fit in brief bursts of activity. Instead of setting aside an hour to go to the gym, you may divide it up into smaller chunks.

Short bursts of activity add up and might help you stay active at home.

An 'exercise snack' is 15 minutes of exercise twice a day on weekdays.

Assume that you work at a desk job and have an hour for lunch. You can undertake moderate-intensity exercise during the last 15 minutes of your lunch break, then repeat it after the workday.

Activity for 15 minutes twice a day, five days a week adds up to... you got it right. — the recommended 150 total minutes of exercise per week.

The concept of 'workout snacks' emerged from the notion of high-intensity interval training (HIIT) and sprint interval training (SIT), in which you strain yourself for a short period, relax for a short period and then repeat. These time-efficient workouts typically last 10 to 25 minutes and have well-established physiological benefits.

Exercise snacks are similar to high-intensity interval training, but with appreciably longer rest periods. Going for a brisk walk, riding your bike, doing a brief aerobic circuit, or even driving a lawn mower are all options.

EXERCISE SNACKING

CHAPTER THIRTY-TWO

FOR INTERNAL PEACE, ONE NEEDS TO LET GO OF MANY THINGS

No matter how flawless one is, how exemplary one aspires to be, no matter how many things we promise ourselves, sometimes whatever we want to achieve just doesn't happen in a day.

IT'S OK. THAT IS REAL LIFE.

Holding on to things, especially negative ones, is like holding your breath.

ONE WILL SUFFOCATE.

In order to move on and before u let go,u must face whatever happened and accept that it is a part of your experience.

Suppression does not work as a long time solution

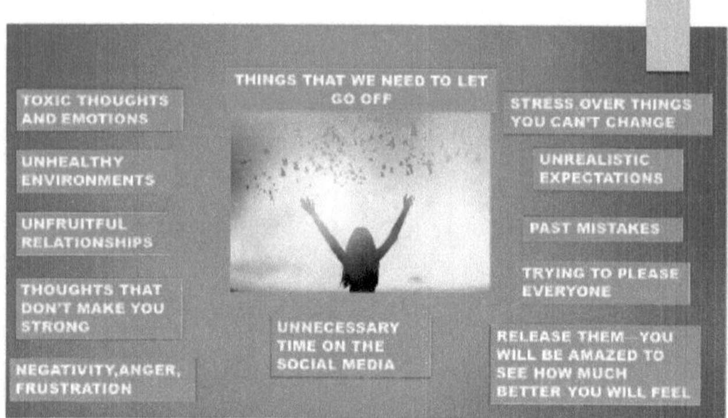
THINGS THAT WE NEED TO LET GO OFF
TOXIC THOUGHTS AND EMOTIONS
UNHEALTHY ENVIRONMENTS
UNFRUITFUL RELATIONSHIPS
THOUGHTS THAT DON'T MAKE YOU STRONG
NEGATIVITY,ANGER, FRUSTRATION
UNNECESSARY TIME ON THE SOCIAL MEDIA
STRESS OVER THINGS YOU CAN'T CHANGE
UNREALISTIC EXPECTATIONS
PAST MISTAKES
TRYING TO PLEASE EVERYONE
RELEASE THEM—YOU WILL BE AMAZED TO SEE HOW MUCH BETTER YOU WILL FEEL

LET GO OF

This was my first attempt at writing and I genuinely hope that the readers will read and appreciate what I have penned down. Even if you can take a tiny tip from my box of tips and can benefit from it then I will be honored.

So I hope you like what you read.

Please get back to me with your views/comments etc.

anjukumaranand@gmail.com

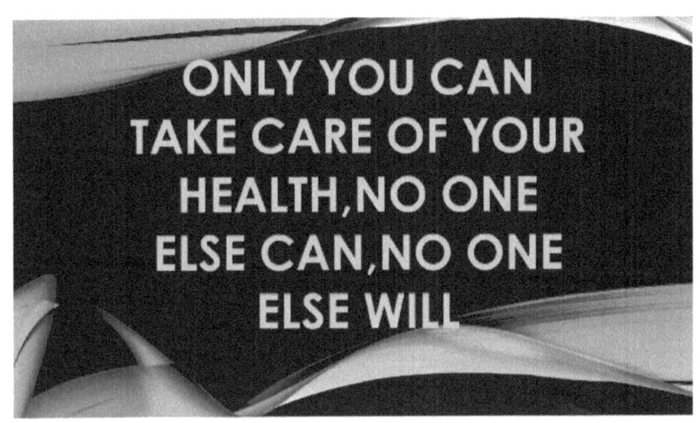

ONLY YOU CAN TAKE CARE OF YOUR HEALTH.

THANK YOU TO ALL